This book is dedicated to my wife
and two children, and to all families
working to find and enjoy their happy way.

Each morning when I rise to find
a sunny day, or no sunshine...

A healthy sleep routine is essential for optimum brain development and emotional regulation in children.

I brush my teeth, and try my best
to think about my night of rest.
Because my bed is wonderful,
and sleep is something beautiful!
I'm thankful for the night of rest.
Now I can be my very best!

 The American Dental Association recommends that children brush their teeth twice a day to maintain good oral health.

For breakfast I am thankful too.
I know breakfast is good for you: some melon,
yogurt, and whole grain bread,
or oatmeal with an apple, and milk instead.

Some eat meat - others won't.
I eat meat sometimes. Sometimes I don't.
An egg is sure to give a boost,
if that's the kind of food you choose.

 Eating a healthy amount of carbohydrates, fats, vegetables, fruits and "protein foods" including meat, seeds, dairy, and legumes is the best way to make sure your body and brain grow to be strong.

With any type of breakfast meal, a glass of water makes you feel like you can handle anything, because you are a living being.

 Dehydration happens when your body has less water than it needs. Urine color is one way to know; pale, clear urine means you are hydrated. Yellow, deep yellow or light brown means you are dehydrated.

Water supports all life, it's true!
Water does a lot for you!

The food you taste and bite - and chew,
has energy that's stored for you.
Water helps unlock the wealth.
Hydration is your key to health!

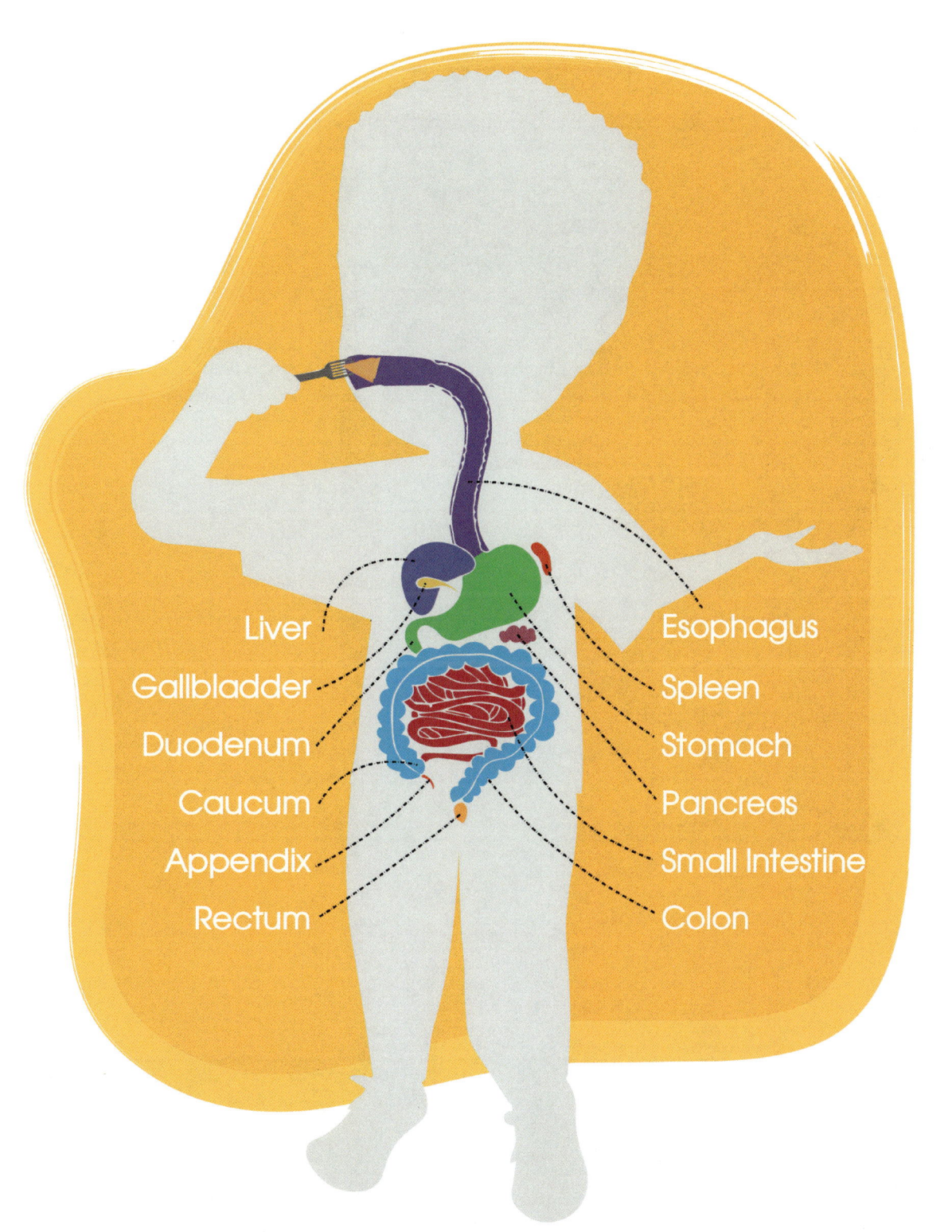

Before you walk out of the door,
what's one thing you are thankful for?

Breathe in deeply through your nose.
Take a pause and hold it close.
And when the air is asking to -
let it out, and then take two
more big breaths just like the first.
(This will feel good when you rehearse.)

And now go back to normal breaths.
You'll feel a calmness in your chest.

 Regular breathing meditation can help improve attention and behavior, counteract some mood disorders, and improve sleep in children.

Picture what you're thankful for.
Now picture it a little more.

Stay with this thought a little while.
This picture is your inner smile.

Now you know a happy way,
to start your morning every day!

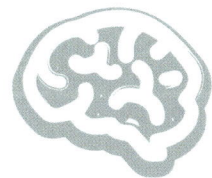

THE HAPPY WAY EVERY DAY!

What are you thankful for?

_____
_____
_____
_____

Draw a picture of your favorite healthy breakfast:

What is your morning ritual?

_____
_____
_____
_____

How do you like to feel right before you leave your home in the morning? Name at least two feelings. (For example: "Alert, and relaxed".)

_____
_____
_____
_____
_____

Think of at least one thing you would like to add to your morning routine.

_____
_____
_____
_____

What time do you usually go to bed at night?

___

What time do you usually wake up in the morning?

___

How do you stay hydrated throughout the day?

___

Draw a picture of you meditating.

Draw a picture of a "happy morning" at your house.

Meet The Author
DAVID STILLS

David is a creative and dedicated educator, performer and writer. He has spent 10 years developing his teaching craft as an early education Montessori teacher, a 4th and 5th grade teacher and most recently as a 6th grade humanities teacher. Prior to teaching, David was an internationally touring vocalist and recording artist. Along with singing, songwriting, and performing (he is currently a vocalist with the Philadelphia-based group, City Love), David is an orator, a writer, and an advocate for diversity, equity and inclusion in education. David is also the author of a chapter in the bestselling anthology, The Guide for White Women Who Teach Black Boys. David is also the author of The Complete Black Man - A set of instructions for a more powerful, truthful, beautiful and fully realized life experience. He is interested in creating works that speak to the experiences of people of color, and that show paths to excellence and prosperity. You can hear David each week on the Instant Grits Podcast. David lives in Glenolden Pennsylvania with his beautiful wife, Melissa, and his two children.

Meet The Illustrator
NICOLE KURTZ

Nicole Kathleen Kurtz is a visual and product designer, with a passion for innovation. Originally from Jenkintown Pennsylvania, Nicole grew up with a love for the visual arts. Nicole graduated with honors from the Savannah College of Art and Design (SCAD), with a degree in Industrial Design. With a portfolio ranging from illustration, graphic design, to product design, Nicole works on every project with a sense of perspective and diverse knowledge. She currently resides in Los Angeles California and enjoys hiking, drawing and baking in her free time.

www.nicolekurtz.com
@nkkdesigns

Made in the USA
Middletown, DE
03 May 2023

29884991R10015